SRA **OpenCourt** **Reading**

Alphabet Book

Mc
Graw
Hill
Education

Bothell, WA • Chicago, IL • Columbus, OH • New York, NY

MHEonline.com

Send all inquiries to:
McGraw-Hill Education
8787 Orion Place
Columbus, OH 43240

ISBN: 978-0-07-669921-6
MHID: 0-07-669921-8

Printed in the United States of America

14 15 16 17 18 GPC 25 24 23

Alphabet Book

Table of Contents

Aa

Ask Anna anything
Ask her, and you'll see
Anna's answers are as good
As anyone's can be.

Anna adds, and Anna reads
And she surely likes to tease.
But all Anna Conda really needs
Are lots of books to squeeze!

Bb

Big, buzzing bumblebees
Bounce from bud to bud with ease.
Big, buzzing bumblebees,
Don't bring your buzz by me
—please!

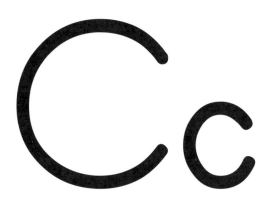

Cc

Can a cold canary sing?

Can a carrot wear a ring?

Can a cow moo when it's mad?

Can a cat frown when it's sad?

Can a castle's candle glow?

Can you tell me—yes or no?

Dd

Doug dared to dig deep.

Dan dug even deeper.

Deon dug the deepest yet

And found a dusty sleeper!

11

Ee

Ten elegant eggs
In a feathery nest,
Ten yellow beaks
Pecked and did their best.

Ten eggshells opened,
And there, in all those eggs,
Were ten baby chickens
And twenty orange legs.

Ff

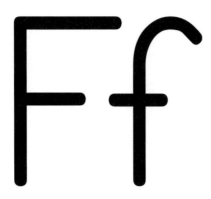

Four funny fishes
Fanned their fancy fins,
Feasted on some fish food,
And licked their furry chins.

Gg

Come into Gabby's garden.

Enter through the gate.

Look at all the good, ripe food

To gather for your plate.

Go get some golden apples,

Picked right from Gabby's trees,

Then get some red tomatoes

And gobble up some peas.

Hh

High up in the hayloft
In a honey-colored hat,
Happy Henrietta Hen
Laid her eggs, then sat.
And sat. And sat.

"Ho-hum," said Henrietta Hen,
"I'm hungry, and I'm hot.
I have to take a supper break,
Then come back to this spot."

Henrietta huffed and hurried
And returned at five 'til six,
And in the honey-colored hat
Were half a dozen chicks!

19

Ii

This little piggy

Likes to spin and stitch,

This little piggy

Likes to dig a ditch,

This little piggy

Likes to lift some bricks,

But this little piggy

Wants to play some tricks.

20

Jj

Julie jumps just for fun,

Jaden jokes with everyone,

Janie judges homemade jam,

Jenna jogs with puppy Sam,

Jordan juggles jacks and toys.

July's a month of jumbo joys!

Kk

Kafi keeps a kettle
Full of special things:
Blue kazoos and kangaroos,
Kittens, kilts, and kings,
Kaleidoscopes and kayaks,
Kickballs, kites, and keys,
Koalas and kimonos,
And seven kapok trees.

Ll

In Latisha's little garden

A lot of flowers grow,

Like lilies of the valley

With blossoms white as snow,

And lavender and lilac

With little purple parts.

Yes, Latisha's lovely garden

Brings beauty to our hearts.

Mm

Monkey, mind your mommy!

Don't mess around at meals,

She made your very favorite:

Some mashed banana peels.

Monkey, mind your mommy!

Be kind and get along,

And when the moon is rising,

She'll hum a merry song.

Nn

Nine nice things are . . .

Happy, happy news,

A brand new pair of shoes,

A nugget made of gold,

A nearby hand to hold,

A little nap at noon,

A napkin and a spoon,

A necklace shining bright,
Twinkling stars at night,
A net of silver strings,
Nine nice things.

Oo

How often have you ever seen

An octopus and otter

Eating olives off a plate

While on a teeter-totter?

Pp

Let's pretend!

Pop like popcorn,

Flip like pancakes,

Sway like palm trees,

Fall like snowflakes,

Peep like peacocks,

Poof like pillows,

Chew like pandas,

Bend like rainbows.

The end!

Qq

"That's quite a quack,"
Said the swan to the duck.
"I'll give you a quarter
If you can also cluck."

The duck got quiet.

He thought for quite a bit.

Then the quacker started clucking

And now he cannot quit!

Rr

A raccoon and a reindeer

Were floating on a raft.

Their lunch fell in the river,

But they only laughed and laughed

Until it started raining,

And then they cried and cried

And paddled for the riverbank

—What a crazy ride!

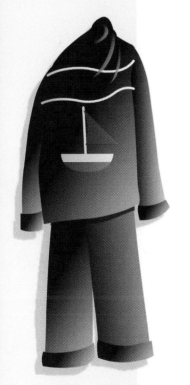

Ss

I see a sub in my tub
And a squeaky, smiling seal,
A seahorse with a saddle
And a sailboat with a wheel.

I know it's kind of silly
To sit and soak and sing,
But a sailor in a bathtub
Can dream most anything.

Tt

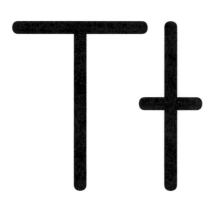

Tutu Tess has tiptoe toes.

She's tall and very sweet.

Tess wears a dress with tiny bows

And toe shoes on her feet.

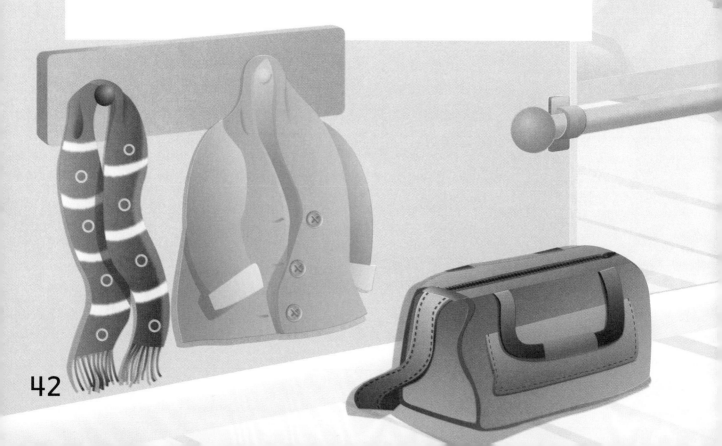

Uu

"Batter up!" called the umpire.

I took the batter's stance

And looked up at the pitcher

Who wore some ugly pants.

Underneath the hot sun

Upon the dusty field,

I swung and missed, one, two, three.

And now my luck was sealed.

Maybe I'm unlucky
Or just a little slow,
My baseball bat was upside-down
—How was I to know?

Vv

We took our family van
To Vermont one day
To a very special market
Not so very far away.

We found a violin,

Some vases and a vest,

A veil made of velvet,

And then we headed west.

Ww

Walruses groan,

Wildcats growl,

Doggies woof,

Wild wolves howl,

Warblers sing,

Woodpeckers pound,

Winter winds wail,

Can you make a sound?

Xx

What's in the box?

Can we x-ray it to see?

It's too small for an ox

And too big for a bee.

Maybe it's a mixer

Or a six-sided stone

Or maybe, even better,

It's a big T. rex's bone!

Yy

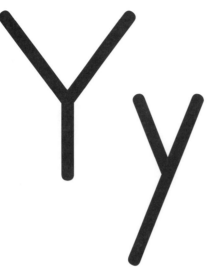

A young yak

With a yellow pack

Walked near and said, "Hello!"

I asked the yak

With the yellow pack

"What's in there? Do you know?"

And he said...

"A yard of yarn,

A sock to darn,

A yo-yo and a kite."

Then the yak

With the yellow pack

Just yawned and said good-night.

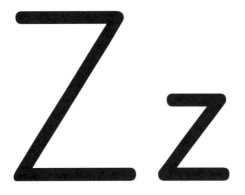

Zz

One day at the zoo

A fuzzy, buzzy fly

Landed on a zebra

And zigzagged by its eye.

The zebra whipped its tail

And zapped the pesky bug

Who zoomed into the air

And landed in a jug.